*gli *speciali*]

i *libri* di **artedossier**

Editorial Manager
Claudio Pescio

Translation
Catherine Frost

Graphics, cover and pagination
Lorenzo Pacini

Picture research
Cristina Reggioli

Imaging editor
Nicola Dini

via Bolognese 165 - 50139 Florence, Italy
piazza Virgilio 4 - 20123 Milan, Italy

First edition: november 2013

www.giunti.it

Reprint	Year
6 5 4 3 2 1	2018 2017 2016 2015

Printed by Giunti Industrie Grafiche S.p.A. - Prato (Italy)

Enrica Crispino

Michelangelo

The Masterpieces

artedossier

DELPHICA

Contents

Delphic Sybil
1508-1512
fresco
Vatican City, Vatican Palaces,
Sistine Chapel

Prisoner or Bearded Slave
c. 1519-1530
marble, height 263 cm
Florence, Galleria dell'Accademia

Opposite page:
Prisoner or Awakening Slave
c. 1519-1530
marble, height 267 cm
Florence, Galleria dell'Accademia

Introduction

Michelangelo lived a long life, remarkably long for his time, traversing over the course of his eighty-nine years different seasons, events and often epochal changes: the beginning of foreign domination in Italy, with the invasion of Charles VIII of France in 1494; the Protestant Reformation, launched by Martin Luther's affixing of his ninety-five theses in 1517; and the terrible Sack of Rome, a traumatic event for all of Christianity, in 1527. Born on March 6, 1475 at Caprese, near Arezzo, this giant of Renaissance art worked with the same tireless energy up to the last days of his life, when, still able to sculpt – sculpture, as he always said, was the art most congenial to him – he continued to work on his last masterpiece, the *Pietà Rondanini*. This long, fascinating adventure is known to us basically by two biographies written during the master's lifetime: one by Giorgio Vasari, published in 1550 (with a second edition in 1568) and one by Ascanio Condivi, from 1553. Condivi, a disciple of Michelangelo's, claimed that his biography was totally reliable, written under the master's direct control. Other information on the artist's life has been found in his letters to family members, with whom he always remained in close contact.

Michelangelo took his first steps as sculptor in Florence, at the Garden of San Marco where, as a talented youth, he learned to use the chisel and studied the ancient works of art collected there by Lorenzo de' Medici. His natural aptitude was soon noted by Lorenzo, who took the young artist into his own home. Brought up with Lorenzo's children, he came into contact with the refined circle of scholars, artists and intellectuals in the court of the Lord of Florence, who initiated him to neoplatonic thought and the cult of the classics. Within a few years' time his career was flourishing, destined to develop in the two main centres of Renaissance Italy, Florence and Rome. At the magnificent papal court of Julius II, the pope determined to restore the Eternal City to its ancient splendour, Michelangelo arrived as an acclaimed artist, after having already sculpted the Vatican *Pietà* and the *David*, to confront, this time as painter, the titanic project of the ceiling of the Sistine Chapel. The ceiling, along with the *Last Judgement*, painted many years later as completion of the Apostolic Chapel, and the *David*, are the works most closely linked to the name of Michelangelo. But his long life abounds in many other masterpieces. Unforgettable are the magnificent sculptures of the Medicean Tombs, the imposing *Captives* and the grieving *Pietà* of his last years. Nor can we forget his brilliant architectural achievements, including his projects for St. Peter's Basilica and the Campidoglio, to mention only the most famous. An all-round artist, he also wrote highly original poetry, verses imbued with intense meditation on death and the torment of his last years.

With his work, Michelangelo left an indelible mark on his time. His influence was to be enormous, not only on the artists of generations to come but also on many of his contemporaries, who were inspired by him and by Raphael to devise a new language distinctive of mid-sixteenth century art, the current that was to become known under the name of Mannerism.

Madonna of the Stairs

Michelangelo's first work, or at least the earliest that has come down to us, shows the influence of Donatello's *stiacciato*, the technique much used by the great 15th century Tuscan sculptor, which consists of conferring a sense of depth and a three-dimensional effect on the figures by barely raising them, leaving them almost flat, as if 'crushed' onto the sculpted surface.
Despite the undoubted technical similarities, however, the differences from Donatello's style are evident. For instance, the strict perspective organisation typical of Donatello's works is absent. This is a significant difference, since it bears witness, along with elements of a different kind, to the profoundly different ideal and expressive values of the two artists. Donatello was, in fact, an artist of the early Florentine Renaissance, the season of reborn faith in the capacities of man, the measure of all things. His works were created at this stage of enthusiasm and certainty, the time when the laws of perspective were discovered and developed. These laws, organising reality according to the measure of human rationality, were to become the founding principle of Renaissance art as a whole. Michelangelo, instead, grew up in the Florence of the Late Renaissance, where the neoplatonic philosophy of Marsilio Ficino brought back to the forefront an approach to reality of the spiritual and religious type. Certainly Michelangelo did not neglect the laws of perspective, now become unescapable, but strict application of them is not one of the salient features of his art. For Michelangelo, the representation of reality was above all symbolical, spiritual and mystic. As compared to Donatello's *Madonnas*, Michelangelo's approach also differs in elements of the composition and iconography. In the first place, in Michelangelo's relief sculpture Mary does not gaze lovingly at the Son she is nursing, but appears lost in her own thoughts; and secondly, the Christ Child is portrayed from the back, in an unusual iconography. Moreover, his muscles seem disproportioned, making him resemble a little Hercules. His twisting body fills the space in a way that seems already distant from typical fifteenth-century art, tending toward solutions that were then to become distinctive of Mannerism. Lastly, there is the element of the stairs, clearly symbolic in meaning. They suggest Ficino's theory of the five degrees of being (five, like the steps carved by Michelangelo) and his scale of love that conjoins the earthly and the divine. A precise reference can be found in a work composed in 1495 by Domenico Benivieni, a friend of the Laurentian philosopher, who in his *Scala della vita spirituale sopra il nome di Maria* (*Scale of spiritual life above the name of Mary*) compares the five letters in the name 'Maria' to the five steps of a stairway.

Madonna of the Stairs
c. 1490
marble, 57.1 x 40.5 cm
Florence, Casa Buonarroti

Battle of the Centaurs

Like the *Madonna of the Stairs*, this is a youthful work sculpted by Michelangelo in 1490-92 (although recent studies seem to show that the artist worked on it again several times, even after 1494, for nearly a decade). It too has been interpreted in a neoplatonic key. According to this hypothesis, it is in fact a 'psychomachia', a battle between the animal and the spiritual sides of the soul. In his biography of Michelangelo, Condivi states that it was Poliziano, an eminent personage in the circle of Lorenzo de' Medici and the tutor of his sons, to suggest the classical subject to the young sculptor, reflecting the typical interest in antiquity widespread in the Medicean cultural sphere. It is probable that Michelangelo was generically inspired by such precedents as the *Battle between Romans and Barbarians* by Bertoldo, curator of the Medicean collections of antiquities in the Garden of San Marco, or by an ancient Roman sarcophagus in the Camposanto of Pisa. But Michelangelo's relief sculpture already shows an intensely personal style and a mature mode of execution, appearing closer to a model chosen entirely independently by the unorthodox young genius, namely the pulpit of Giovanni Pisano in the Baptistery of Pisa. The subject of that work, recalled by Condivi as the 'Abduction of Deianira and skirmish of the centaurs', seems to have served the young sculptor mainly as inspiration for a thorough study of the nude figure. And the tangled bodies portrayed in every pose furnished the artist an inexhaustible repertory to draw on throughout his career. For the background left indefinite and the absence of a frame, the *Battle of the Centaurs* can be considered the first of Michelangelo's *non finito* works. Condivi, who mentions it as a work completed at the death of Lorenzo the Magnificent, in April 1492, fails to explain whether the *non finito* effect was purposely decided by the artist, or whether it is due to his having suspended the sculpture at the death of Lorenzo, when the disconsolate Michelangelo left Palazzo Medici to return to his father's home.

Bacchus

This statue was sculpted during Michelangelo's first stay in Rome, after his arrival in the city of the popes in 1496. It was commissioned by Cardinal Raffaele Sansoni Riario della Rovere, nephew of Pope Sixtus IV and client of the banker Jacopo Galli, an enthusiastic patron of the young artist. When the work was finished, however, the cardinal refused it, perhaps because the statue did not appear classically balanced as in the ancient figures of *Bacchus* it was supposed to emulate. Its swaying figure, instead, clearly expressed the god's state of drunkenness; and a *Bacchus* who was obviously drunk might be seen as an embarrassing allusion to the orgiastic atmosphere of the Borgia pope's papal court. And so the statue was purchased by Galli, who placed it in the garden of his home, a real outdoor *antiquarium* filled with works of ancient (as well as 'modern') art. A drawing made by the Dutch artist Maarten van Heemskerck between 1532 and 1535 bears witness to the collocation of the *Bacchus*, the most exceptional piece, and also shows the damage undergone immediately by the statue, whose right hand is missing. It was reintegrated later, along with the cup it holds. For Michelangelo this sculpture was the chance to measure himself against antiquity, drawing inspiration from a vast range of statues and relief carvings (where Bacchus frequently appears in wavering balance) and in particular, as the most likely model, a gigantic portrait/statue of Antinous – the Emperor Hadrian's favourite – with the attributes of a god, then to be found in the Farnese Collection. The final result is a totally original sculpture in which Vasari, in agreement with other contemporaries, saw a certain ambiguity, noting "both the slenderness of a young man and the fleshiness and roundness of a woman".

Bacchus
1496-1497
marble, height 209 cm
Florence, Bargello National Museum

Opposite page:
Battle of the Centaurs
1490-1492
marble, 80 x 90.5 cm
Florence, Casa Buonarroti

Pietà

The typology of the Virgin holding her dead Son in her lap derives from a Nordic model, not particularly widespread in Italy but known to artistic circles (as shown by the *Pietà* of Ercole de' Roberti, of Perugino and of Francesco Botticini) and through small wooden statues designed for private devotion. Of the known examples in Italy, the statue in St. Peter's Basilica is the monumental version, transposed into marble. This sculpture was not only the first highly important commission assigned to Michelangelo but also the only work he ever signed. His signature, in fact, appears on the band running across the Virgin's breast, where the words «MICHAELA[N]GELUS BONAROTUS FLORENT[INUS] FACIEBAT» can be seen. The client for this famous marble group was the French Cardinal Jean Bilhères de Lagraulas, Ambassador of Charles VIII, King of France, to Pope Alexander VI. The Cardinal signed the contract in 1498 with the intermediation of Jacopo Galli, the banker who had been one of the artist's first admirers and patrons in Rome.
The *Pietà* was originally destined to the cardinal's tomb in Santa Petronilla, an Early Christian chapel annexed to Constantine's ancient basilica, destroyed to build the new St. Peter's, where Michelangelo's masterpiece would then be placed. It is hard to say with certainty exactly where the group was originally positioned, since over the centuries it has been moved several times within the basilica; its present collocation dates from 1779. It may be assumed that Michelangelo intended to position it so that the Virgin's face would not appear in a frontal view but – in keeping with the movement of her head bowed over her Son – would be half-hidden.
Vasari and Condivi had noted the distinctive features of this superb work. On the one hand, the sculptor's *bravura*, the technical virtuosity that indulges in a minute, impeccable rendering of anatomical details; and on the other, the serene beauty of the figures – most notably, the gentle and surprisingly young Virgin – and the poignant aesthetics of marble statuary as lustrous as alabaster, so finely has the stone been smoothed and polished. Never again in the production of this master of the *non finito* are we to find a work so pristine, so finished, sculpted it might seem to demonstrate having attained a formal goal from which then to depart. As further proof of his mastery, Michelangelo carved the *Pietà* from a single block of marble, adding no supplementary pieces. He chose the block himself in the quarries of Carrara, supervising its transport to Rome in a journey lasting nine months.
In Michelangelo's masterpiece Mary, absorbed in quiet grief, contemplates with lowered eyes her dead Son deposed from the cross. Her right hand firmly supports the Divine body, touching it only through the shroud it is wrapped in, while her left hand opens out in a gesture that seems to bring the onlooker into the tragedy and mystery of the Redeemer's sacrifice.
As regards composition, perfect equilibrium has been attained between the two originally contrasting volumes. On one side is the Virgin, seated and erect; and on the other Christ, whose nude body, stretched out in his Mother's lap, is so finely balanced by the ample drapery in the lower part of the Virgin's dress that the two figures seem inscribed in a single compact block. And here Michelangelo splendidly transcends the rigidity of the northern model, where the contrast between the two bodies remains accentuated. In the Vatican *Pietà* instead, the Mother and Son are fused in a pyramidal construction that is a monolith of quiet suffering perfectly contained within itself.
Today as yesterday (as shown by Vasari's criticism) the Virgin's extreme youth is disconcerting. Unusual in representations of this kind, it is unrealistic when seen in relation to Christ's age at his death. No certain reason for this is known, but according to Condivi's biography, Michelangelo declared that chaste women remain young longer than others; as if to suggest that Mary's purity is translated into visual terms by her enduring youthfulness.
The *Pietà*, completed in only one year, was finished in that same 1499 that marked the death of its client. In 1972 a psychopath managed to strike Michelangelo's masterpiece repeatedly with a hammer, damaging it at various points (the Virgin's left arm was broken off, her nose and eyelids seriously impaired). The damage was immediately restored, making use of the numerous plaster casts existing, with excellent results.

Pietà
1498-1499
marble, height 174 cm
Vatican City, St. Peter

David

In 1501, at the age of twenty-six, Michelangelo was commissioned by the Florentine Republic to sculpt a great statue portraying David, the young shepherd destined to become King of Israel, the Biblical hero who defeated the giant Goliath.
The enormous block of Carrara marble assigned to Michelangelo for this project had already been extracted many years before and had attracted the interest of the Florentine governors, who had considered having it sculpted into a statue on several different occasions. In 1464 the undertaking had been entrusted to Agostino di Duccio, but the contract had then been cancelled for unknown reasons. Then in 1475 the commission had been assigned to Antonio Rossellino, who only roughed out a statue without completing it. At the time when Michelangelo accepted the commission, the block of marble was lying abandoned in the storehouses of the Opera del Duomo, the institution responsible for architectural and decorative works in the Florentine cathedral, which had been completed over half a century earlier by Brunelleschi's miraculous dome. Since the gigantic statue was in fact destined to adorn one of the buttresses of Santa Maria del Fiore, it had to be an imposing sculpture that could be easily seen from below. Michelangelo engaged to finish the statue in two year's time, for a salary of six gold florins a month. But the project took more time than expected, both because the undertaking was in itself arduous and because the sculptor preferred to work alone, without assistants; other problems then, were involved in working on a project already begun by others rather than on virgin material. In 1504 the statue was finally ready. A monumental sculpture of this size had never been seen since antiquity. It is amazing, then, to think that Michelangelo sculpted it in a makeshift workshop, set up haphazardly in the vicinity of the Cathedral, where he laboured night and day, frequently sleeping only a few hours on the floor and never leaving his work.
The *David* immediately appeared so grandiose and magnificent that its first destination now seemed inadequate. The question arose as to where this masterpiece could best be placed, and to decide this a commission was set up, whose members included such great figures in the world of art as Leonardo da Vinci, Giuliano da Sangallo and Filippino Lippi. In the end, it was decided to place the giant, with its intense civil significance, in Piazza della Signoria, centre of the city's political life. David, who had fought for the freedom of his people, incarnated to perfection, in fact, the symbol of republican virtue. But new questions arose as to its exact positioning: under the Loggia dell'Orcagna (later known also as the Loggia dei Lanzi) or, as others proposed, clearly in view before Palazzo della Signoria, the solution that was then adopted. The original of the *David* remained standing before the Palazzo until 1873 when, to protect it from the weather, it was moved to the Tribune in the Galleria dell'Accademia, specially designed to hold the masterpiece, where it still stands today. In Piazza Signoria it was replaced by a copy only in 1910.
As concerns iconography, Michelangelo's *David* is a notable departure from the Florentine precedents of Donatello and Verrocchio. The *David* of Donatello, in fact, wears boots and

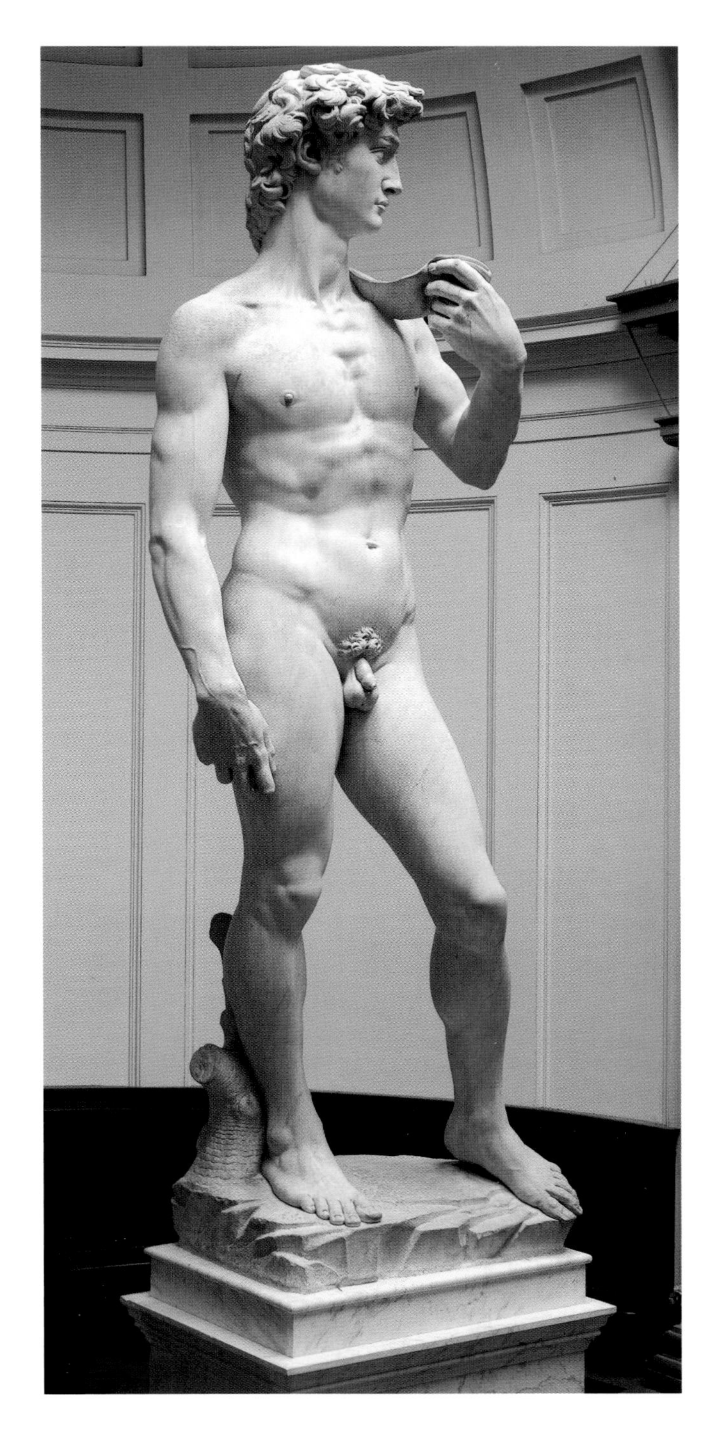

David
1501-1504
marble, height 517 cm
Florence, Galleria dell'Accademia, Tribuna of the David

Opposite page:
Tribuna of the David at the Galleria dell'Accademia
post 1903 - ante 1909
Florence

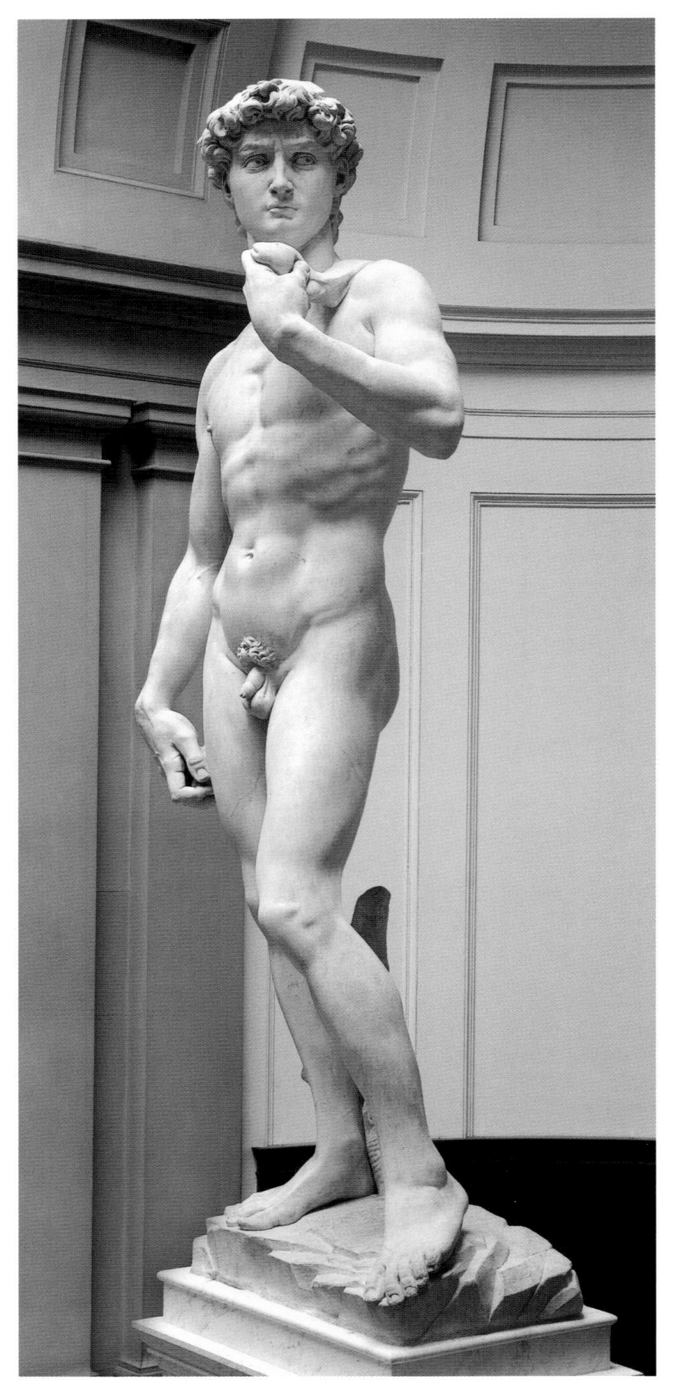

a helmet and carries a sword. The hero envisaged by Verrocchio also has a sword and boots and wears a light gown, in keeping with the Biblical text. Their bodies are slender and adolescent; at their feet lies the severed head of Goliath. Michelangelo's *David* is instead nude like a Greek god, carrying only a slingshot over his left shoulder. His body is that of a young man, and his heroic feat has not yet been accomplished (Goliath's head is missing). Michelangelo portrays him just before the struggle, visualising the tension of this moment in the taut face, the concentrated gaze and the muscles ready to spring into action. This pose seems to have been a well-meditated decision of Michelangelo, considering that the documents on the *David* state that the artist was first asked to adorn the hero with a garland of gilt leaves and a gilt belt, in keeping with more traditional representations. Instead the sculptor clearly modelled his *David* on a classical statue, although it is impossible to specify any precise model. In doing so, he renewed the dictate of the contemporary sculpture of the time where, as was happening in other fields, the 'modern' was expressed through a deliberate and original retrieval of the past.
Unlike Donatello's *David*, splendid as it is, Michelangelo's masterpiece is equally magnificent when viewed from all sides, not from the front alone. The technique and execution appear perfect, which is even more remarkable considering the size of the statue. As in all of Michelangelo's sculptures, his knowledge of the human body is exceptional, and the rendering of anatomical details impeccable. The study of anatomy, another of the innovations that marked a significant change in Renaissance art, was a requisite that Michelangelo was to share with another genius, one whom he always opposed, Leonardo da Vinci. The latter took his anatomical studies so far as to practice the dissection of cadavers (uncommon at the time), and was actually accused of sorcery for this reason.
In this masterpiece, the subject of the highest admiration for over five centuries, even the presence of an 'error' in one of the wrists manages to serve a purpose from the artistic point of view. The sculptor adds a muscle, in reality non-existent (one of the very few anatomical inexactitudes found in Michelangelo's work) but which contributes to heightening the overall effect of plasticity.

The Dying Slave and the Rebellious Slave

Known by these names since the 19th century, when they were interpreted in a highly romantic key, the two sculptures were originally planned for the monumental complex with the long and tormented history that was to be the Tomb of Pope Julius II. According to the contract stipulated with the pope's heirs in 1513, as previously mentioned, the statues now in the Louvre were intended to appear on the papal tomb in the guise of 'Captives', a subject that Michelangelo found highly stimulating for its great expressive potential. The sculptor developed the theme by creating powerful figures, contorted in grief, undoubtedly influenced by the famous models from antiquity well known to him, such as the *Laocoön*, which he had seen in person at the time of its discovery in 1506, and the *Belvedere Torso*.

The languid, sensual beauty of the *Dying Slave* and the position of its raised arm recall the iconography of the martyrised St. Sebastian. Around the chest and at the wrists the figure is bound by bands often interpreted as chains, although they do not seem to hinder its motion. The monkey holding a mirror barely roughed out behind the legs seems to authorise Condivi's interpretation of the *Slaves* as figures symbolising the arts (which ape nature by imitating it) and which have fallen into slavery after the death of Julius II.

While the *Dying Slave* seems to slide gently downward under the weight of his own lassitude, the attitude of the *Rebellious Slave*, with hands tied behind his back, stretched forward in virile struggle, is instead firmly energetic. His sinuous, powerful body, in a pose of 'opposition' between the left shoulder and the right knee, expresses all the tension of a completed motion. The right shoulder, however, is flat and undefined, perhaps because the sculpture was designed to be placed on a corner of the funerary monument.

Donated by Michelangelo in 1546 to his friend Roberto Strozzi and brought by the latter to France, the *Slaves* then entered the Louvre when they were purchased by the museum in 1794.

Dying Slave
c. 1513
marble, height 229 cm
Paris, Musée du Louvre

Opposite page:
Rebellious Slave
1513
marble, height 215 cm
Paris, Musée du Louvre

Moses

In the group of sculptures for the Tomb of Julius II, completed in 1513, the only work entirely by the hand of Michelangelo is the *Moses*, a sculpture of exceptional impact for its power and vigour, intensified by the 'terribleness' – a Michelangelesque attribute par excellence – of its gaze. The figure is powerfully dynamic, with that abrupt sideways turn of the head and the left leg stretched tautly back, only the toes touching the ground, as if Moses were about to leap suddenly to his feet. This impression is heightened by the fact that such a sudden movement would have let the Tables of the Law, resting on the seat, slide to the floor and to keep them from falling, Moses tightens his right arm around them. The horns on the prophet's head represent the continuation of an erroneous translation of the Biblical text. The appellative 'cornutus' is in fact a translation of the Hebrew word for 'radiant' and refers to the passage in *Exodus* describing Moses descending from Mount Sinai carrying the Tables of the Law, with two bands of light beaming from his head. An example of the highest virtuosity is the beard, its curling locks so finely carved as to cause Vasari to exclaim that it seems more "a work of the brush than of the chisel". But as an exhibition of *bravura*, there is even more. During restoration of the funerary monument, concluded after five years of work in 2003, a document was found. According to it, Michelangelo, when he positioned the sculpture on the final monument between 1542 and 1545, thirty years or so after its completion, made some modifications. The most striking of these is the twisting of the head, reworked at this time and turned to one side, as seems confirmed by other indications emerging during the restoration.

Moses
1513
marble, height 235 cm
Rome, San Pietro in Vincoli

Medicean Tombs

This famous sculptural-architectural work of Michelangelo is one of the projects commissioned by Pope Leo X Medici for San Lorenzo in Florence, the church that fell under the patronage of the pope's family, being located in the 'Medicean quarter' (around the splendid residence that Michelozzo had built for Cosimo the Elder).
In 1520 Pope Leo X, with the support of Cardinal Giulio de' Medici – who was himself to become pope in 1523 under the name of Clement VII – asked the artist to construct a new family chapel in the church, modelled on the first chapel/mausoleum in the Old Sacristy built by Brunelleschi between 1421 and 1426. Giovanni di Bicci, father of Cosimo the Elder, and the sons of the latter, Piero and Giovanni de' Medici, had been buried in Brunelleschi's sacristy, in a chamber decorated by such artists as Donatello and Verrocchio. In like manner, the tombs of Lorenzo the Magnificent, his brother Giuliano, and the younger members of the Medici family who died prematurely during those years – Giuliano Duke of Nemours (son of Lorenzo the Magnificent and brother of Pope Leo X) and Lorenzo Duke of Urbino (the pope's nephew) – were to be placed in the chapel now commissioned of Michelangelo. And so the New Sacristy was built, as a *pendant* not only ideal but also physical (inasmuch as being placed at the opposite end of the transept) of Brunelleschi's Old Sacristy. Accordingly, the New Sacristy reflects the structure of the old one, with a square floor plan, domed ceiling and pietra serena ribbing. However, the chamber designed by Michelangelo is a much more tensely dramatic ensemble, striking in its complexity; an evocative place where architecture and sculpture join hands, breathing life into an enigmatic symbolic itinerary, whose definitive significance is still subject to debate among art historians today.
As for other works by this incomparable artist, here too an interpretation in the neoplatonic key is the most plausible. According to this interpretation, the ensemble of the New Sacristy should be seen as an image of the universe with the three superimposed spheres of the underworld, the human and terrestrial world, and the celestial vault above. From their sepulchres the souls of the deceased, entrusted to the allegories of Time and of the Rivers (the latter then not realised) would rise to eternity, symbolised by the Virgin.
Unfortunately, however, only two of the planned tombs were competed, those of the Medici family's younger generation, the two dukes. As idealised rather than realistic figures, Lorenzo Duke of Urbino is portrayed in a meditative pose (Vasari called the statue "Il Pensieroso"), while Giuliano Duke of Nemours is modelled after the statues of Roman emperors, wearing armour and carrying the sceptre of command. Each tomb is adorned by two allegorical statues, which are among Michelangelo's most extraordinary works. On the sarcophagus of Giuliano are *Night* and *Day*; on the tomb of Lorenzo, *Dawn* and *Dusk*. The *Virgin and Child* situated on the opposite side of the altar is also by Michelangelo. This sculpture stands over the simple sarcophagus containing the mortal remains of Lorenzo the Magnificent and his brother Giuliano, assassinated in the Pazzi Conspiracy of 1478; beside it are the statues of the Medici family's patron saints, Cosmos and Damian (sculpted by two of the master's pupils, Giovanni Angelo Montorsoli and Raffaello da Montelupo).
The plans also called for Michelangelo to sculpt four allegorical statues of the *Rivers* (of the Other World) to be placed on the floor, plus another four figures to fill the niches at the sides of the dukes' tombs. None of these works was realised. The project remained unfinished both for political reasons (the new expulsion of the Medici and consequent restoration of republican government to Florence as a repercussion of the Sack of Rome in 1527) and for the personal vicissitudes of the artist, who left Florence permanently for Rome in 1534. The task of definitively arranging the chapel then fell to Giorgio Vasari and Bartolomeo Ammannati, who finished the work in 1554-1555.

Night,
detail of the Tomb of Giuliano de' Medici, Duke of Nemours,
with allegories of *Night* and *Day*
c. 1526-1531
Florence, San Lorenzo, New Sacristy, Medicean Chapels

Page 24:
Tomb of Giuliano de' Medici, Duke of Nemours,
with allegories of *Night* and *Day*
c. 1526-1531
Florence, San Lorenzo, New Sacristy, Medicean Chapels

Page 25:
Tomb of Lorenzo de' Medici, Duke of Urbino,
with allegories of *Dawn* and *Dusk*
c. 1525-1527
Florence, San Lorenzo, New Sacristy, Medicean Chapels

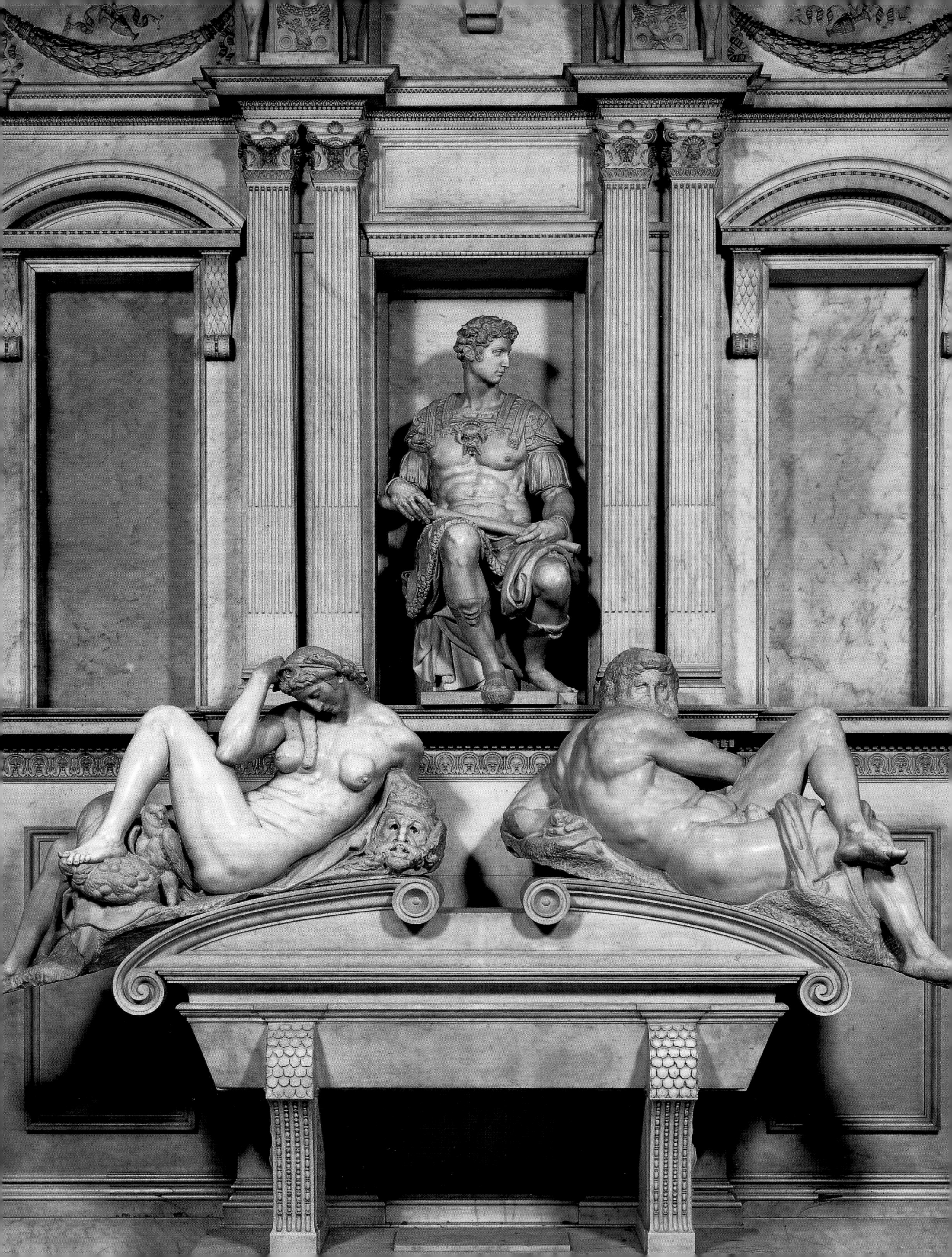

Prisoners

In 1519, a year before beginning work on the New Sacristy for the church of San Lorenzo in Florence, Michelangelo began to sculpt the statues of four *Prisoners*. They were destined to the endless work in progress that was the tomb of Pope Julius II, for which a new contract with major changes had been stipulated in 1516. Due to the many commitments assumed by the artist during that period, the sculptures remained in the rough-hewn state, much less highly finished than the two splendid *Slaves* sculpted earlier for that same tomb, the *Dying Slave* and the *Rebellious Slave*, which however, like the other four, were never used for it.
But the fascination of the *non finito* – whether deliberate or not as the case may be – that fully reflected Michelangelo's thoughts on sculpture as the process of freeing form from matter, enucleating an idea already present in the block of marble, emanates imperiously from the nude statues of the *Prisoners* emerging from the stone as if they had lain captive within it.
At the death of Michelangelo in 1564, the *Prisoners* had remained in the artist's Florentine studio, in Via Mozza. His nephew, Leonardo Buonarroti, then donated them to Grand Duke Cosimo I de' Medici. Subsequently, in 1586, the sculptures were placed at the order of Francesco I, Cosimo's son, in the park of the Pitti Palace – the Boboli Gardens – in a fascinating setting: the Large Grotto designed and built by Bernardo Buontalenti between 1584 and 1587. There they remained until 1908 when, for obvious reasons of conservation, they were replaced by plaster casts and moved to their new home in the Galleria dell'Accademia of Florence to lead the way to the Tribune and the *David*.

Opposite page:
Prisoner or Awakening Slave
c. 1519-1530
marble, height 267 cm
Florence, Galleria dell'Accademia

Prisoner or Atlas
c. 1519-1530
marble, height 277 cm
Florence, Galleria dell'Accademia

Below:
Prisoner or Young Slave
c. 1519-1530
marble, height 256 cm
Florence, Galleria dell'Accademia

Prisoner or Bearded Slave
c. 1519-1530
marble, height 263 cm
Florence, Galleria dell'Accademia

Tomb of Julius II

In 1505 Pope Julius II summoned Michelangelo to Rome, requesting him to design his mausoleum. This was the first act in the long, tormented history of planning and realisation that dragged on for forty years, during which the project for a grandiose monument to be placed in St. Peter's Basilica was progressively transformed into a much more modest work, abandoned by Michelangelo to a host of assistants and finally relegated to the secondary church of San Pietro in Vincoli. In the absence of the first contract, the original idea for the mausoleum may be hypothesised on the basis of the sources (Condivi and Vasari, although frequently discordant), according to whom the plans called for a monument with four 'faces', a majestic mausoleum modelled on ancient examples, standing free on all four sides and adorned with forty statues. This model was repeatedly reduced over the years to less imposing versions, becoming in the end a simple 'backdrop' standing against a wall, with no more than seven statues and only one of them, the magnificent *Moses*, carved entirely by the hand of Michelangelo.
The course of the project, amid quarrels, sometimes violent, first with the pope himself and then with his heirs, modifications and interruptions in the work, is summarised in the words of Michelangelo himself, who called it the "tragedy of the tomb". The first project dating from 1505 was never even begun. It was followed in 1523 by another contract stipulated by the heirs of Julius II after his death. It differed from the previous one basically in a modification that was to be retained to the end, consisting of backing the tomb up against a wall and eliminating the funeral chamber – designed to hold the pope's sarcophagus – placed inside the structure in the first project (Julius II was not, in fact, buried here but in St. Peter's Basilica beside his uncle Pope Sixtus IV). It was at this time that the *Moses* was sculpted for the Tomb, as well as the two *Prisoners* known as the *Rebellious Slave* and the *Dying Slave* – now in the Louvre –which were then not utilised.
After this, four more contracts were signed: one in 1516 (a version calling for four more *Prisoners*, sculptures that remained in the rough-hewn state and are now at the Galleria dell'Accademia in Florence); another in 1526 (project rejected by the clients for unknown reasons); a third in 1532 (changing the destination of the monument to the church of San Pietro in Vincoli; dating from this time is the sculpture of the *Genius of Victory* now in Palazzo Vecchio, Florence); and the last in 1542 (when the clients agreed to let the work be completed by assistants, but under the guidance of Michelangelo).
The funerary monument to Julius II was finally completed in 1545, appearing almost as a monumental 'facade' enlivened by a number of statues. Something very different indeed from the original ambitious project.

Tomb of Julius II
completed in 1545
marble
Rome, San Pietro in Vincoli

Pietà Bandini

In his last years Michelangelo returned to the theme of the Pietà in deeply grieving accents far removed from the composed suffering of his youthful *Pietà*, reflecting a tormented existential state marked by obsessive reflection on the subject of death and afflicted by profound religious perturbation. On the iconographic level too, the *Pietà* of the artist's mature years differ from the statue in the Vatican. Christ's body is no longer stretched out in his mother's lap, as if cradled by the Virgin, but is portrayed in the vertical position, sinking heavily downward and supported with visible effort. Here the model that served as inspiration is probably to be found in the painting of the Veneto region, in the *Pietà* of Giovanni Bellini and of Mantegna, where Christ's body is displayed almost as a monstrance.
The *Pietà Bandini,* named for Francesco Bandini who was its owner almost up to the end of the 17th century, was sculpted by Michelangelo between 1550 and 1555. According to Vasari, Michelangelo first planned to use the sculpture for his own tomb, which he wished to have placed in the church of Santa Maria Maggiore in Rome (the artist, who died in the papal city, was instead buried at Santa Croce in Florence, where his body was brought in secret by his nephew Leonardo). The personage of Nicodemus, the hooded figure who is supporting Christ, is according to tradition a self-portrait of Michelangelo. The work was voluntarily damaged by the sculptor who, dissatisfied with it, broke off the Redeemer's right arm with a blow of the hammer. Later one of his pupils, Tiberio Calcagni, reintegrated the missing arm and completed the group, sculpting entirely the figure of Mary Magdalene. However, he did not attempt to finish Christ's left leg, which has remained mutilated.

Pietà Bandini
1550-1555
marble, height 226 cm
Florence, Museo dell'Opera del Duomo

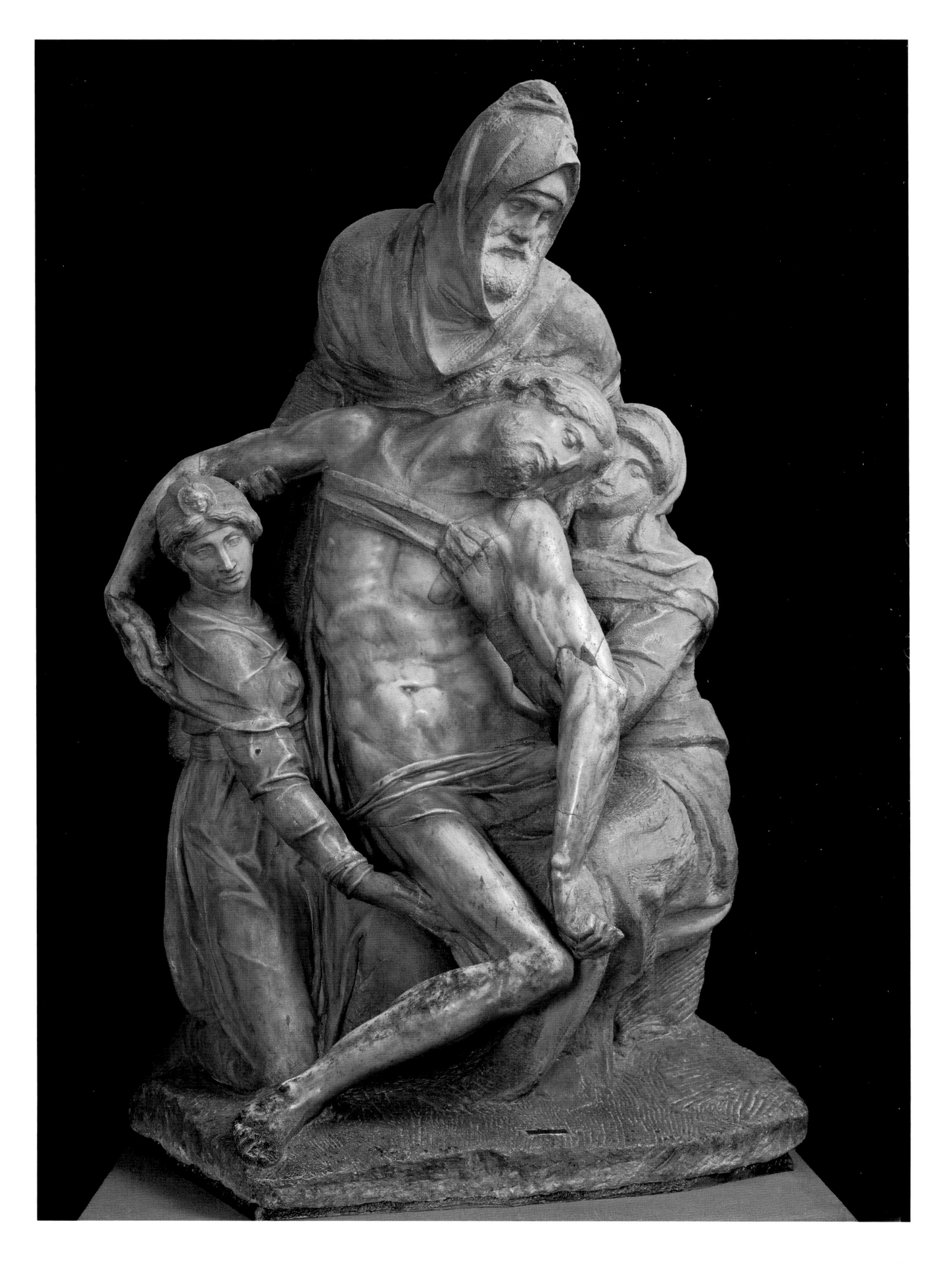

Pietà Rondanini

Named for the Rondanini family, who owned it for years and from whose palazzo in Rome it comes, this is Michelangelo's last achievement, the sculpture he continued to work on up to the evening before that February 18, 1564 when death overcame him; an almost incredible feat, when we think that at the moment of his death the artist was eighty-nine years old. Michelangelo worked on the statue in several different stages, as shown by the numerous corrections and modifications, some quite drastic. The most evident trace is the surviving stump of Christ's right arm, beside the new figures. The shape and size of the limb seem to indicate that it comes from a first version, dated around 1552-1553, in which the bodies were not so emaciated but probably had more 'classical' proportions. In the second version, begun in 1554, the spectrally slender figures and the *non finito* effect, so amazingly attuned to modern taste, confer on the group great dramatic impact and an intensely spiritual aura. In the extreme abandonment of Christ's dead body, in the manifest effort exerted by the Virgin to support him, we no longer find the serene composure and harmony emanating from the Vatican *Pietà*, but instead grief and desperation, freely displayed. And not this alone. The pathos of the *Pietà Rondanini* is even more agonising because it is mingled with tenderness, the loving gesture of a mother seeking almost to gather unto herself, in a last desperate attempt to protect Him, the Son that Michelangelo sculpted as if embedded in the Virgin's body.

Pietà Rondanini
1552-1564
marble, height 195 cm
Milan, Castello Sforzesco

Doni Tondo

The Holy Family of the *Doni Tondo* was painted for Agnolo Doni and Maddalena Strozzi, perhaps on the occasion of their wedding, celebrated in 1503-1504, or a few years later, in 1506-1507; in any case, around 1506, the year when another great artist of the time, Raphael, painted splendid portraits of the husband and wife.
The composition on a circular support falls within the most typical Florentine fifteenth-century tradition, as exemplified by Botticelli's *Madonna of the Pomegranate* and Luca Signorelli's *Madonna of Humility*, paintings whose influence on Michelangelo is clear, although not strikingly evident. In the *Doni Tondo*, in fact, Michelangelo's tendency to experiment is already accentuated. In the first place, the iconography of the group is unusual, with the Madonna twisting on herself to receive her Son from the arms of St. Joseph, who is passing the Child over her shoulder. Equally unusual is the figure of the Virgin. Mary has strong, sturdy features and is portrayed without a veil and wearing a sleeveless gown of classical style that seems to anticipate the *Sibyls* painted on the ceiling of the Sistine Chapel.
And then there are the colours: cold, clear, shimmering and crudely juxtaposed, a chromatic choice that preludes to the palette revealed by the latest restoration of that same chapel, and that sharply contrasts with the taste of the times, attuned to a pleasing harmony of tones. The young nudes in the background also evoke the Sistine Chapel, resembling the *Ignudi* on the famous ceiling. Already in the *Doni Tondo*, as later in the masterpiece frescoed in the Vatican, Michelangelo's figures seem almost like painted sculpture, with the *Holy Family* in the Uffizi painting showing a marked three-dimensional effect, its powerful sculptural impact heightened still further by the sharp contrast between light and shadow.
As regards meaning, the Florentine painting seems to allude to the division of humanity before and after the birth of Christ. If this is the case the nudes, appearing behind the low wall that divides the Holy Family from the youths in the background, are not classical-style shepherds as in Signorelli's painting, but probably represent the pagan world before the Revelation. Still belonging to that world is John the Baptist, the child St. John who significantly leans against the wall, and is the only one shown gazing toward the protagonists of the New Testament.

Tondo Doni (*Holy Family*)
1503-1507
oil on panel, diam. 120 cm
Florence, Uffizi Gallery

Ceiling of the Sistine Chapel

The need to fresco the ceiling of the Sistine Chapel again had arisen due to damage in the old decoration observed starting from 1504, when a large crack had opened in the ceiling. Michelangelo, his thoughts absorbed in planning the pope's tomb, grudgingly accepted the commission assigned him by Julius II in boundless trust of the artist's capabilities, considering that he had furnished little proof so far of his talent as painter.
The iconographical program originally agreed upon was quite simple, with the twelve Apostles in the vaulting cells and the lateral spandrels, and a simple architectural decoration in the central band. Instead, on a vast surface of over five hundred square metres, the master's incomparable brush delineated – in only four years of back-breaking work, from 1508 to 1512 – the history of mankind from the primordial chaos to the promise of Redemption: a grandiose prologue to the coming of Christ, animated by some three-hundred-and-thirty-six figures, a perfect ensemble of sculptural volumes and brilliant colours in a framework of illusionistic architecture that seemed to open to the outside, free from the iron rules of Renaissance perspective.

Michelangelo claimed authorship of the entire concept. However, its complexity, not merely formal but also as regards content, suggests a collaboration between the artist and the erudite theologians of the papal court, who probably suggested themes and ideas that were then developed by the artist in his own manner. Among the names proposed by scholars are the Franciscan Marco Vigerio and Egidio da Viterbo, who had been a pupil of Marsilio Ficino in Florence. And, in fact, a reading in the neoplatonic key has prevailed among the critics, although a recent proposal for interpretation sees the frescoes in relation to Savonarola's sermons.

As regards the subjects, the central band on the ceiling is formed of nine panels frescoed with stories taken from *The Book of Genesis*. They were painted starting from the entrance to the chapel, while the chronological-narrative order begins on the opposite side, with three scenes from the Creation (*Separation of Light and Darkness*; *Creation of the Heavens*; *Separation of Land from Water*), followed by another three scenes representing the *Creation of Adam*, the *Creation of Eve*, *Original Sin*, and three stories of Noah (*The Sacrifice of Noah*, *The Flood*, and *The Drunkenness of Noah*). Five of the nine episodes are smaller in size, with at the

Brazen serpent,
Prophet Ezekiel
and, on opposite page,
Ignudo
1508-1512
fresco
Vatican City, Vatican Palaces,
Sistine Chapel

Pages 34-35:
Ceiling of the Sistine Chapel
1508-1512
fresco
Vatican City, Vatican Palaces

corners, in dynamic poses, pairs of nude male figures (the famous *Ignudi*) holding bronze medallions with stories taken from the Biblical *Book of Samuel* and *Book of Kings*. In the side panels around the middle band are depicted seven *Prophets* and five *Sibyls* – each with the name written on a plate held up below by a cherub – who, although pertaining to the pagan world, were deemed to have been among those who heralded the coming of Christ. In the vaulting cells and lunettes, Michelangelo then painted the *Ancestors of Christ*, from Abraham to Joseph. Lastly, in the lateral spandrels – surmounted by bronze-like nudes frescoed also at the tops of the vaulting cells – appear four scenes from the Old Testament, highly significant episodes in the history of Israel that allude to the messianic promise: *The Bronze Serpent*, *The Punishment of Aman*, *David and Goliath*, *Judith and Holofernes*. Restoration of the ceiling, completed in the late 1980s, has brought to light the original colours of the frescoes, which had been dimmed for centuries by dirt and soot. Clear, cold, transparent colours, anti-naturalist colours (totally different, for example, from those of the contemporary sixteenth-century Venetian masters), colours "of the soul", already experimented in the *Doni Tondo* and heralding the Mannerist palette to come.

Creation of Adam,
Original Sin and Banishment from the Garden of Eden
1508-1512
fresco
Vatican City, Vatican Palaces, Sistine Chapel

Last Judgement

It was Pope Paul III, the former Alessandro Farnese, who commissioned Michelangelo to realise a project that had already been planned by his predecessor, Clement VII Medici. It called for continuing the decoration of the Sistine Chapel, which had begun with the frescoes on the ceiling, completing it with a grandiose *Last Judgement* on the wall behind the altar. In 1536 then, twenty-four years later, the artist came back to paint in the Sistine Chapel. To make room for the new fresco, three works by Perugino and other artists in the existing fifteenth-century decoration had to be destroyed, as well as two lunettes that Michelangelo himself had painted in 1512 as conclusion to the work on the ceiling.

Michelangelo illustrated the theme of the *Last Judgement* with an anthology of superb scenes and unforgettable figures, inspired in part by Dante Alighieri's D*ivine Comedy*.

The composition is roughly divided into three bands, one above another, crowned at the top by two lunettes framing wingless angels who bear the symbols of the Passion. In the lowest band of the painting are portrayed, at left, the resurrection of the dead at the end of time, at right, Hell with Caron in his boat ferrying the souls of the damned and Minos intent on judging them. In the middle band, at the centre, appears a group of angels with the trumpets of Judgement Day, while on the left the Blessed rise to the kingdom of Heaven and on the right the Damned fall into the infernal flames. Lastly, in the top band, the majestic figure of Christ the Judge, with the Virgin at his side, is surrounded by a throng of the Elect.

In comparison to the traditional Italian iconography for this subject, as had been handed down up to then, the critics are unanimous in deeming Michelangelo's Judgement totally innovative. Not only is the arrangement of the figures different (especially as concerns the angels with the instruments of martyrdom and those with the trumpets), but the composition is not arrabged in clearly distinct bands, but instead conveys the impression of a maelstrom aroused by the raised arm of Christ, a vortex of Cyclopean figures suspended in clusters and not set in any precise compositional scheme. Recent contributions, however, have demonstrated that the typology of the Sistine fresco lies within the northern tradition of representing the *Last Judgement*, as shown by comparison with the painting of Rogier van der Weyden in Beaune (1443-1451), an iconographical model probably known to Michelangelo through Buffalmacco's fourteenth-century fresco in the Camposanto of Pisa.

The *Last Judgement* was completed in 1541. Michelangelo began to paint the fresco starting from the top, from the lunette on the left, and continuing in orderly manner toward the bottom.

Prior to the restoration conducted in 1990-1994, the surface of the fresco appeared heavily soiled. By bringing back to light the bright, luminous colours, the restoration has entirely discredited the long-held view of the work as a shadowy masterpiece where the terrible nature of the subject seemed to find expression in the dark, sombre colours. In some of the figures, tradition has it that Michelangelo portrayed contemporary personages. St. Peter is said to bear the features of Pope Paul III; Minos those of Biagio da Cesena, as the artist's revenge for some criticism of the painting expressed by the Master of Ceremonies; and St. Bartholomew is said to be a portrait of the writer Pietro Aretino, while on the flayed skin of his martyrdom, which the saint holds in his hand, Michelangelo is thought to have painted his own self-portrait.

In 1545, four years after the unveiling of the *Judgement*, Pope Paul III convened the Council of Trent, an attempt by the Church of Rome to react to the advance of the Protestant Reformation. Consequent to the decisions taken by the Council, which closed in 1563, a wave of intransigence swept through the countries that had remained Catholic, and censorship struck even at the nudes in the *Judgement*, now deemed obscene. This decision dates from January 1564. Michelangelo died a month later, on February 18. The job of covering the 'scandalous' nudity of his figures was given to his friend and pupil Daniele da Volterra, 'Il Braghettone', as the artist was then called due to the 'braghe', or pants, that he used to cover the nude figures painted by the master, completed the work in 1565, intervening 'a fresco' on some of the figures, such as *St. Biagio* (whose head was turned in another direction) and *St. Catherine* (who was 'dressed'), originally represented crouching one above the other in a position judged equivocal.

Last Judgement
1536-1541, whole and detail of *Christ the Judge*
fresco
Vatican City, Vatican Palaces, Sistine Chapel

IONAS

Angels Carrying the Signs of the Passion,
St. Bartholomew
1536-1541
fresco
Vatican City, Vatican Palaces, Sistine Chapel

Next page:
The Haughty (or Damned for Desperation),
Arrival of the Damned in the Underworld
1536-1541
fresco
Vatican City, Vatican Palaces, Sistine Chapel

Medicean Laurentian Library

In Florence, again for the San Lorenzo complex, Michelangelo received another highly important commission from Pope Clement VII Medici, who soon after his election in 1523 asked the artist to design the Laurentian Library, to house the precious Medicean collection of codices and manuscripts. Work on the library started in 1524 but, as in the case of the New Sacristy, it remained unfinished at the time of Michelangelo's definitive departure for Rome in 1534 and the death of the pope. It was only under Cosimo I, between 1548 and 1571 (the year when the library was opened to the public), that the project was completed, based on the drawings and rare indications of Michelangelo, by such outstanding artists as Niccolò Tribolo, Giorgio Vasari and Bartolomeo Ammannati. Upon entering the first area of the Laurentian, the so-called *ricetto* (vestibule), the impression is that of entering a courtyard closed off by the facades of four palaces. This is due to the utili-

Laurentian Library, Vestibule
1524-1571
Florence, San Lorenzo complex

Laurentian Library, Reading Room
1524-1571
Florence, San Lorenzo complex

sation, in an interior, of such exterior elements as windows and columns. The ensemble, vigorous and dynamic, is distinguished by a marked vertical aspect in contrast to the horizontal development of the second area, the reading room, to which the *ricetto* is connected by a monumental stairway with a central flight of elliptical steps and two lateral flights with squared steps. Up this magnificent stairway, originally designed by Michelangelo in walnut but then built of pietra serena in 1559 by Bartolomeo Ammannati to a model by Michelangelo himself, visitors pass from the half-shadow of the vestibule to the reading room flooded with light, in a continuation of the contrast between the two rooms. The library is divided by two rows of benches, the famous *plutei*, also designed by Michelangelo, for the reading and safekeeping of manuscripts. He designed the ceiling too, carved by Giovanni Battista del Tasso and Antonio di Marco di Giano, known as Carota, in 1549-1550.

Campidoglio

Commissioned by Pope Paul III Farnese, Michelangelo designed and supervised the remodelling of Piazza del Campidoglio, starting in 1538. This was a real urban renewal plan, beginning with the design – for the first time in Rome – of a public space based on a detailed preliminary project. Michelangelo retained the two existing buildings, the medieval Palazzo Senatorio, to which he added a monumental double-ramp stairway, and the fifteenth-century Palazzo dei Conservatori. To them he added a third building, the Palazzo Nuovo (now the seat of the Musei Capitolini), in order to close the square on three sides like a horseshoe. He then renovated the facades of the existing buildings and, applying a scenographic perspective stratagem that anticipated urban planning trends of the following century, oriented the two side buildings along slightly diverging axes, opening out like scissors from the central edifice, Palazzo Senatorio. Lastly, in the middle of the square, on a base designed by him and decorated with the Farnese lilies, he placed a splendid ancient statue, the equestrian monument to Emperor Marcus Aurelius (thought at the time to represent Constantine) which Paul III had ordered brought here from the Lateran.

At the centre of the open side of the square, Michelangelo designed a long, monumental stairway providing easy access to the newly designed piazza. The artist did not live to see his project completed. It was finished, with some changes in the original plan, by Giacomo della Porta and Girolamo and Carlo Rainaldi, and was not fully completed until the second half of the 17th century. And in fact, the paving designed by Michelangelo, with the ornamental motif of stars formed of intertwined ellipses enclosed in an oval shape, was finished only in 1940.

Dome of St. Peter's Basilica

Perhaps the most prestigious Roman project of Michelangelo as architect – a commission he voluntarily accepted entirely without recompense – was the continuation of the work of rebuilding St. Peter's Basilica. The rebuilding had begun in 1506 at the order of Pope Julius II and had involved the progressive demolition of Constantine's old basilica dating from the 4th century. Appointed in 1546, at the age of seventy-one, Director of the Fabric of St. Peter's, Michelangelo utilised with some variations the idea of the central plan proposed by Bramante in the past, designing a majestic dome to crown the basilica, inspired by the double-shell structure erected by Brunelleschi for the Cathedral of Florence but of much more imposing size. Highlighted by the return to the central plan and by Michelangelo's new stratagems for intensifying its impact, the dome represented the symbolic, as well as the architectural culmination of the new St. Peter's Basilica.
Michelangelo died when the dome had been constructed only up to the tambour. It was then finished with some variations from the original concept. The first projects show, for example, that the trabeated windows were a solution adopted only later, after the original motif of the oculi. A wooden model of the dome exists, although it does not faithfully reflect the original project. It was in fact built when work on the tambour had already begun, was probably subject to modifications that changed its original appearance, and was not in any case binding for the execution of the work, since Michelangelo claimed for himself the right to decide, for the entire basilica, on any changes he might deem suitable.
The dome was completed, between 1588 and 1590, by Giacomo della Porta and Domenico Fontana, who gave it a more elongated shape than the planned version, which may have been perfectly spherical. Today it remains the element that, more than any other, bears traces of Michelangelo's project for the basilica, extensively modified by Carlo Maderno in the 17th century.

Opposite page:
Campidoglio
1538-1564
Rome

St. Peter's Dome
1546-1564
Vatican City

Photography credits

Archivio Giunti:
photo Antonio Quattrone, Florence: 14-17; Rabatti & Domingie, Florence: 6-11, 22-27, 30-31, 33, 44s

Archivi Alinari, Florence:
32d; Per concessione del Ministero per i Beni e le Attività Culturali: 44-45; © René-Gabriel Ojéda/CNAC/MNAM / RMN-Réunion des Musées Nationaux: 18-19

Courtesy of the Fabbrica di San Pietro in Vaticano: 13

Foto Musei Vaticani: 4, 34-43

© Luigi Nocenti/Olycom: 32s

© 2013 Foto Scala, Florence - su concessione del Ministero per i Beni e le Attività Culturali: 20-21, 29

© Anibal Trejo/Shutterstock: 47

© Giovanni Simeone/Sime/Sie: 46

The publisher is willing to settle any royalties that may be owing for the publication of pictures from unascertained sources.